CONTENTS

Step 3: VISION — ENVISION YOUR NEW LIFE
Life begins when abundance is irrelevant

SOMETIMES IT DOES TAKE A BRAIN SURGEON

BRIAN E. WAGNER

AUTHOR ACADEMY elite

Printed in the United States of America

Published by Author Academy Elite
P.O. Box 43, Powell, OH 43035

www.AuthorAcademyElite.com

Paperback: 978-1-946114-62-4
Hardcover: 978-1-946114-63-1
Library of Congress Control Number: 2017905484

FOREWORD

As a mentor to thousands of authors, speakers, and coaches, it takes something special to catch my attention. I've met people from every walk of life. And although everyone is uniquely created, Brian is definitely an outlier.

If you look at him on the outside, you might not be impressed. He's an average guy. But it's what he has on the inside that impresses me time and time again.

The guy is a ball of fire. He's an action-taker and an unstoppable force. He's insanely curious and committed to growth—more than most.

I think he's tremendously successful simply because he just won't quit. Some call it tenacity. Others call it grit. He doesn't believe in the word *losing*.

If I give him a challenge, he does it every time. He's not afraid of failing or risking or believing. He takes imperfect action on a regular basis.

He does laps around people who trust in talent because Brian believes in something better—effort.

I'm honored to write his foreword. I believe in him and the value he brings. Although he might not be the most polished author who ever wrote a book, pay attention to him and his words. His content is gold and his approach to life is even more valuable.

If you can replicate even half of Brian's enthusiasm, you will multiply your impact 10x.

This is your moment.

This is your legacy.

It's time to address your blind spots and embrace a radical vision.

—Kary Oberbrunner, author of *ELIXIR Project, Your Secret Name, The Deeper Path,* and *Day Job to Dream Job*

A portion of the proceeds from this book will go directly to A Kid Again. This charity focuses on helping not only sick children, but their entire families. A Kid Again looks forward to the day that every child with a life-threatening illness in America can be A Kid Again. They include the whole family in every adventure hosted year-round. Families say the adventures are something positive to look forward to, and that they offer a distraction from routine medical care. Whether a child is battling an all-too-common disease like cancer, or a rare disease like Hunter syndrome, they ALL deserve to be a kid again.

ENDORSEMENTS

Vision is a true superpower and Brian shows us not only how to develop it, but truly harness it to face diversity, overcome obstacles, and create lasting positive change. Brian has an extraordinary story that can help even the most ordinary of us see more possibility in our lives and the lives of everyone around us.

—Mark Henson
founder, sparkspace
author, *Ordinary Superpowers*

In this book, Brian has simplified what he has gone through in questioning, identifying and charting a vision for a better life.

He will help you delve into your own known or unknown blind spots and using specific tools for B.L.I.N.D., S.I.G.H.T., and V.I.S.I.O.N. help you to be more, achieve more and SEE more of what life has to offer.

—Jon Petz
Motivational Keynote Speaker & Emcee

INTRODUCTION

What Happened

I used to remember things in reference to significant events in my life. My marriage, the birth of my children, the Buckeyes' National Championship...

Times have changed. Now every day is a new life. When I wake up and am able to see the alarm clock, I'm happy. Blowing my nose means I'm breathing; sneezing is exciting. Swallowing my food without a feeding tube makes me giddy. Seeing my children is the greatest activity I know.

My wife is my life.

While my full story starts on July 11, 1967, the day I was born, that date is also the origin of what happened to my vision many, many years later.

My mom and dad had no idea that I was born with defects in the middle of my brainstem. Neither did Connie Brueggemeier when I asked her to be my wife in September of 1990. During the course of my adolescence, there had been definite signs, but nothing was pinpointed until 1992 at the University of Chicago Hospital. That's when a diagnosis of multiple cavernous malformations was given. At that point, no prognosis or exclusions were given. I went on living my normal life with my new bride, and began raising a family that includes three amazing children.

That normal life changed in October of 2010. When I began seeing double and my eyelids started drooping uncontrollably, I was told that the cavernous malformations had bled or moved. Despite these alarming symptoms, the doctor was adamant about one potential treatment, telling me, "*Never* let anyone operate on your brainstem." I was given steroids and, by mid-November, my eyes returned to normal.

Life went on. My wife, Connie, and I took a trip to Cancun for our 20th anniversary, and everything was wonderful. In February of that year, I even bought a new car. I would drive that car for just three weeks before my last trip with two good eyes.

That's when, on March 3, I went to Cleveland for sales training. During the course of the day, I noticed that the PowerPoint presentations were becoming doubled on the screen. When the day was over, I walked to my car and gingerly drove out of the parking garage. During the drive home, I had to stop several times. I called home to tell my wife what was going on and that I would try to get some rest — maybe the symptoms would go away. They never did. Several hours later, I arrived home safely, where I flopped on the couch. At 3:00 in the morning, I woke up and went to go upstairs to bed. On the way, I stopped for a look in the bathroom mirror. **For the first time, I saw the person that I am today — on the outside.**

After the kids were off to school, we went to the ER. When the testing was over, the doctor came in and said, "You're going to want to consider someone operating on your brainstem. Your conditions will only get worse as the bleeds of the cavernous malformation become more frequent. We have three options for surgeons in this field; the best option is in Arizona." My wife and I both felt our hearts sink into our stomachs; my world started spinning out of control as I was admitted to the hospital. That evening, Connie and the kids came to visit me. I think they were much more nervous than I was. At that point, when I saw my kids, I heard a clock start ticking. It was a clock that I heard day and night from that point on.

While Connie filled out the necessary forms and gathered medical records, I waited and grew increasingly worried about further bleeding. Connie sent the records to the "rock star" doctor in Arizona with money for processing and a commitment that we weren't using him for a second opinion. The doctor and staff in Arizona had to review my case and determine whether I was a candidate for surgery. I didn't know what I would do if he didn't accept me, so we went to the third choice at the Cleveland Clinic. The doctor seemed very knowledgeable and indicated that they perform a couple of these surgeries a year. However, he told us that he knew of the doctor in Arizona, and said that if he were in my shoes, he would want Dr. Spetzler (yep, the "rock star" doctor) to operate. Now, as they say, all we could do was wait.

Most mornings, when I was lucky enough to forget about the ticking clock inside my head, I was reminded that I couldn't open my eyes enough to see the alarm clock on the nightstand beside me. For the next month, I was forced to tilt my head back and look out of a slit that formed where my eyelid was not completely covering my eyeball, just at the bottom of my eyes. Maybe, if the surgeon in Arizona accepted me as a candidate for surgery, I would be able to see again.

Finally, the call came from Barbara at the Barrow Neurosurgical Institute at St. Joseph's Hospital, saying Dr. Spetzler would see me. We were ecstatic. If I could've seen Connie's raised hand, we would have given each other a high-five. As it was, we just held each other and cried with joy.

The next two weeks were the longest days that I can remember, as we waited for my surgery date in Phoenix. The words "worse" and "more frequent" kept going through my head. "What if?" I thought. I drank to forget, and I prayed to remember. I wanted to forget the "what ifs" and remember how to feel normal again.

On April 1, I was wheeled into surgery, given sedation medication and told to count backward from 10. "Ten, nine, eight…." Then my head was bolted into a metal halo to prevent unwanted movement. Scars from those bolts would stay with me for a long time.

The surgery was flawless; I was able to walk the halls that same afternoon and was discharged the next day!

My checkout was on Saturday, April 2. That afternoon, like many to follow, I napped after lunch and took a leisurely walk with Connie.

During the next month, my left eye started to open. My right eye did not. When my right eyelid is forced open, my vision is double.

Whenever I would come downstairs in the morning, I'd ask my youngest son, Colin, if he could tell a difference. *Were my eyes becoming more opened?* Without fail, he'd look at me and say, "yeah, I think so." He was 11, but he gave encouragement that I valued like it came from an 80-year-old.

Six months after my operation, my vision hadn't changed, and neither had my faith. The way that people react to my face is striking. My portal to the world cuts out a lot of "noise" and shows people for what they are. Now, all of my meetings are intentional. There are no occasions that don't matter.

After my surgery, Connie was telling the kids about how I was disappointed that the surgery didn't fully correct my condition. My youngest son took the phone and said "patience, grasshopper." Where did he get that? I forgot to tell you that we have a lot of humor in our family. Then on Father's Day, my daughter handed me a card with this note:

Dear Dad,

Happy Dad's Day! I hope you have a great day because you definitely deserve it. This font is for you. It's called "You're loved." I picked it because it describes you perfectly. All the cards and TV commercials always say, "My dad's the best!" But they're all lying! You're the best ever. Sure, other people's dads are great. They're younger than you, sportier, funnier. [author's note: where is she going with this???] But you've got something they don't have. Bravery. Even after everything you're going through, you still get out of bed in the morning. You still joke around. You still go out and play with us and cook on the grill, even though you only have half of one good eye! Through all that, you still put a smile on lots of people's faces. Especially mine. But you do more still!! You inspire me. You teach me that even if you go through everything, believe that everything turns out okay in the end, believe that sometimes, that the only thing that you can do is hope beyond hope, then maybe, just maybe, you'll make it out alive. Not always unscathed, but alive. And giving me that hope, that sense of belief, well, I'd take that over a dad with two good eyes any day.

Love, love, love, love, love, love
Jess

Just when you think that you're not having an impact on people, you can be surprised. I was putting on a strong face for my family and people, but what they were seeing is hope and direction.

Regardless of my condition, I am blessed to be here today. There are many of you that would give anything to have a loved one back in most any condition. While it's true that I've become more of a burden to many people, I hope that my positive attitude and impact outweighs that burden.

After all, I am alive.

I went blind, but my vision is better now than it's ever been. My new vision is to help as many people as I possibly can to clear any obstacle that they have in front of them.

Sometimes it DOES take a brain surgeon.

3 STEPS TO CLEAR ANY OBSTACLE

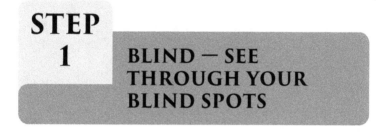

STEP 1

BLIND — SEE THROUGH YOUR BLIND SPOTS

BLIND SPOTS CONNECT OUR PAIN TO OUR POTENTIAL

CHAPTER 1

QUESTION YOUR VIEWS — SEE FROM ANOTHER PERSPECTIVE

We are all living in a dream, but life ain't what it seems
— Imagine Dragons, Dream

*C*rash.

Something bad is bound to happen if you consistently fail to check your blind spot when you're driving. Although my use of the phrase "blind spot" has a slightly different meaning, it still has the same intent as the one that we find in the dictionary. As Merriam-Webster puts it, a blind spot is:

> **1a :** the small circular area at the back of the retina where the optic nerve enters the eyeball and which is devoid of rods and cones and is not sensitive to light — called also *optic disk.* **b :** a portion of a field that cannot be seen or inspected with available equipment

2: an area in which one fails to exercise judgment or discrimination

When we're driving, we can see forward through our windshield. With the use of our mirrors, we can see behind us. However, much like in life, we still can't see what is in our blind spot. If the government legislates that the automotive industry address this vulnerability in our cars, why aren't you looking into your own blind spots? Maybe you're just taking it for granted that there's nothing in them to obstruct your journey.

I used to take walking down a sidewalk for granted — until I couldn't see it clearly anymore. A common, everyday activity was suddenly a challenge for me. I had to study the sidewalk more intently for uneven slabs and crumbled corners that could trip me.

Once I paid attention to it, it was no longer a challenge, but once again something I could navigate safely. Life is full of blind spots, and paying closer attention to what's happening around you can help you. It's looking through the blind spots that could put you on a path to your potential. But in order to do that, you need to recognize your blind spots, and that requires looking at yourself from a different perspective.

> Life is full of blind spots, and paying closer attention to what's happening around you can help you. It's looking through the blind spots that could put you on a path to your potential.

Sometimes you're forced into having a different perspective due to a life-altering event. However, wouldn't it be nice if you could change your perspective without such a high cost? Why does the cost of admission have so much to do with the value seen on the other side of the door?

You actually know what it's like to be blind. We all have been blind at one point or another. Blindness comes in many forms; we can be blinded by greed, anger, ignorance, frustration, lust, or power. The list is seemingly endless.

When you succumb to one of those feelings, you are blind.

In the past, I wasn't one to think about my life too much. Deep thoughts were usually lost on me. I never got the "moral of the story." I never thought that I had blind spots. When people said, "he doesn't know what he doesn't know," I thought it was funny just because of how it sounded.

In March of 2011, my blind spots became huge. In fact, I was totally blind. Both of my eyelids refused to open. The only way I could see light was if I lifted one of my lids with my finger. Blindness can mean different things to different people.

But it doesn't take physical blindness to have blind spots. There may just be something that you do that draws a negative reaction

> It doesn't take physical blindness to have blind spots.

from others. What's more is that you don't always know that you do it. You aren't annoying or hurting them on purpose.

So, what are these blind spots? They can be broken down into three categories.

- Obvious — I can see it, but it's not a problem to me
- Grievous — I can't see anything, but I notice people are treating me differently
- Oblivious — "I hear nothing, I see nothing, I know nothing!" — Sergeant Shultz, Hogan's Heroes

Obvious blind spots

Obvious blind spots are the ones that you choose to ignore. It doesn't matter to you how other people receive your message — it's all about you. You may have to step on a few people to get what you want, but that doesn't seem to bother you.

These are blind spots that require intentional addressing. They come from your thought processes and require you to change them. This isn't always easy to do, but it is certainly necessary.

As I sit here writing this book, I'm choosing to ignore the fact that we need to have more income to support our family. The current situation is not sustainable and will eventually be rectified. We're not really "stepping on" anyone, just asking them to wait while this season of life passes us by.

You have to know something about the expected outcome of your situation. You'll need to have a plan in place to rectify the issue. The tool that can be used to combat Obvious blind spots is what we call an O.P.U.S. This will be discussed, in depth, in the later chapters of this book.

Grievous blind spots

The Grievous blind spots are much more serious and severe.

When you have these blind spots, you're setting yourself up for failure. The first domino in a chain reaction will determine the fate of the remaining dominos. For example, sometimes we all get into too much of a hurry. We know that we need to be somewhere, and we know when. However, we don't always know the *how*. If we just started walking down the sidewalk without determining which direction we should be going, that would be grievous. Trust me, I've done that and ended up walking in circles.

In a recent trip to downtown Columbus, I parked my car in what I thought would be an appropriate spot. Google Maps indicated that I was very close to my final destination. When I made my way to the sidewalk, I suddenly realized that the exact location wasn't exactly clear. I went to the right and started to look for address numbers on buildings and street signs. Even when I'm walking, those darn numbers are hard to see!

Next street, right turn. Next street, right turn. Before you know it, I'm back to where I started.

Let's go left this time. Boom. The building suddenly appeared.

When I first started down this sidewalk, I made the decision to go right, and as I continued along, the ramifications of my decision were exacerbated. It wasn't until I took a few more right turns that I was able to begin rectifying my initial wrong turn as I came back to my starting point.

When you have a Grievous blind spot, you'll need to ask for help *before* you need it. This is a difficult blind spot to see through, but you can do it if you reach out for help. If there's one thing that can be learned in going through difficult times in life, it's that you can't do it alone.

Get a coach. Have a mentor. Sit down and have an intentional meeting to create actionable outcomes.

Oblivious blind spots

Oblivious blind spots are much like Obvious blind spots, the exception being that the oblivious ones are not as easily discerned.

As adjectives, the difference between *oblivious* and *obvious* is that *oblivious* (usually followed by "to" or ''of") means "lacking awareness; unmindful; unaware, unconscious of," while *obvious* means "easily discovered, seen, or understood; self-explanatory."

Oblivious blind spots are the ones where you need the most help, either because you don't realize you have them, or because you are pretending they don't exist.

Here's how being B.L.I.N.D. can be used as a tool for you to see from another perspective. Once you have that perspective, things will begin to appear to you that you have never seen before.

Remember, we don't need our eyes to see.

Belief. In *As a Man Thinketh*, Napolean Hill writes, "watch what you think about, because your thoughts will become your words." Your belief system will set your course for your life.

An easy way to determine your "beliefs" is to look at what you are consuming. This goes far beyond food and drink. We're also consuming music, television, books, social media, podcasts, newspapers, and magazines. On top of that, consider the relationships that you have. This is also a form of consumption. What is your belief system? Do you even know what you believe in?

We can all share our belief system, but we can't give it to someone. You believe what you believe. I believe what I believe. Convincing and selling each other on our ideas is possible, but the other person will most likely revert to their former belief. That is, of course, unless the other person is truly changed.

However, you can impact the other person in a positive way for the future. You may never know the impact that you're having. But, rest assured, you will have an impact.

Lesson. During the course of the day, we have hundreds of opportunities to learn lessons. Turn right at the Starbucks, not left. Leave your keys in the same place every day; that way you'll always know where they are. If you're leaving your car outside, don't leave your windows down.

You can even learn a lesson during a stroll down the sidewalk. This used to be a much simpler thing for me. Who wouldn't take it for granted? Being more reflective after that walk downtown, there are lessons to be learned that we'll talk about in this book.

Some people miss the best lessons in life. They think that they're learning during the good times. In actuality, you're learning the most during the times that you failed.

What I've come to find out is that the most beneficial and long-lasting learning comes from failure. That sidewalk may take different turns. It may have peaks and valleys. You may even run into someone along the way. You see, this is where it becomes personal. Failure has the effect of internalizing the learning in a unique way, especially after you run into enough people or wrench your back from a missed step.

My dad used to say, "if you're not making any mistakes, it's because you're not doing anything." This reminds me of a famous quote:

"It is not the critic who counts; not the man who points out how the strong man stumbles, or where the doer of deeds could have done them better. The credit belongs

9

to the man who is actually in the arena, whose face is marred by dust and sweat and blood; who strives valiantly; who errs, who comes short again and again, because there is no effort without error and shortcoming; but who does actually strive to do the deeds; who knows great enthusiasms, the great devotions; who spends himself in a worthy cause; who at the best knows in the end the triumph of high achievement, and who at the worst, if he fails, at least fails while daring greatly, so that his place shall never be with those cold and timid souls who neither know victory nor defeat."

— Theodore Roosevelt

It gives me chills every time that I read it. I like to read it out loud with passion. Doing that brings it to life, much like how Teddy would have read it. This creates a desire in me to continue to take imperfect action. It creates a passion for success even at the price of experiencing failure. The times that we'll be able to accomplish something of substance on the first try are rare.

Investment. If you're going to do something, do it right or don't do it at all. Have you heard that saying before? I know I have. If it wasn't from my dad, it was from one of my brothers. Growing up with seven older brothers and two older sisters didn't leave me much room for error. There was always someone telling me that this should be done differently or that I was healthy enough to go to school or work in the field. On our tomato farm in Northwest Ohio, our family raised 350 acres of tomatoes and a thousand or so acres of each field corn and soybeans. My childhood growing up wasn't always fun and games. It ended up being a lot of hard work — when they made me. I was the baby, after all.

Usually, when *investment* is mentioned, we tend to think of financial investment. That's only one component, though. Think of the other forms of investment.

- Emotional — This requires deep thought at times. Sometimes it's a matter of having the clear, uninterrupted air to spend time with your own thoughts. It's at times like this when you are able to do your best work.
- Time — It's the only resource that can't be created. You can "make" time, but not without "destroying" the time for something else. We all have the same 86,400 seconds in a day. It's all about what you chose to do with them.
- Self-education — What are you doing to better yourself? Are there classes that you can take on Saturdays? How about nights and some of those personal days that haven't been used? I'm willing to bet you that there are options available. If money is an issue, there are remedies for that. Library cards are free. Many people have taken internet-based free classes, sometimes through the library or universities.
- Social Networking — This means disconnecting from your devices (think more than just smartphones) and connecting on a human level. Delete applications that distract you from your core. How do you know what your core is? We'll get to that in Chapter 11.
- Sacrificial — When I started writing this book, I realized that I would have to sacrifice a great deal in order to complete it, not to mention to even get started. You may have to sacrifice time with friends,

relaxation hours, television shows and movies to accomplish a goal of this size.

This process of writing a book has served as a constant reminder that in order to make money, you have to spend money. Unfortunately, spending time doesn't mean that you're making time, so spend it wisely. Those two sentences right there should be the only thing that you need to help you determine which is more important to you.

Necessary. Blind spots are a necessary part of who you are. You'll see more clearly when you embrace them. If we weren't made to have them, don't you think that God would have made us with eyes in the back of our heads? There have been many times that those blind spots have helped to show more than the naked eye could see. It's amazing how many times people who are close to me have told me that I have a blind spot. Not only does it help me with the current situation, but it also allows me to rely on them more in the future. It's at times like those that you realize whom you can trust and have faith in.

Decision. The Latin word *decision* literally means "to cut off." Making a decision is about "cutting off" choices — cutting you off from some other course of action. Now that may sound a little severe and limiting, but it's not. It's liberating.

You see, having many choices is great; but at some point, if we're going to get to where we want to go, and if we're going to attain what we want to attain, then we need to make some decisions.

Don't view making a decision as a debilitating thing. It's not actually "cutting you off," as the root of the word may suggest. In fact, making a decision frees you from the shackles of endless choices so that you can get to where you want to go. Then, once the decision has been made, commit to it. But that doesn't mean that you shouldn't question it from time to time.

Think of the word B.L.I.N.D. as a tool for helping you to see through your blind spots. This should help you to see the world from a new perspective.

CHAPTER 2

QUESTION YOUR PATH —
SEE WHAT YOU'VE
BEEN MISSING

Sometimes you have to lose everything to see anything.

I fell.

Just as I was approaching the end of a 3-mile run, the sidewalk monster grabbed me by the ankle. It was one of the parts of the sidewalk that was sticking up. I was feeling the effects of the run — burning lungs and legs that felt like wet noodles. Home was only a block away. The beautiful, sunny, crisp morning was blotted out in a heartbeat.

It had been six years since my surgery, and I hadn't fallen once since then. This time, I fell hard.

It seemed like it was over before it started. My proverbial ride high upon the seat of someone who calls himself a "runner" (even though no one else would even dream that was the case), came quickly to an end. It all came crashing down with 197 lbs. of 49-year-old flesh. It culminated in a slide that would have made Pete Rose proud.

"Safe!" At least that's probably what Pete would have heard. "Out!" was all that I could think.

Fortunately, I careened off the sidewalk and into dewy grass for my Hall of Fame (or not) slide. I may have eaten a little grass and soaked up a little mud, but I felt like I was still okay. Without hesitation, I stood up and looked around. Apparently, no one had seen me. Then I heard a car go by, but wasn't able to see it. I'm sure that they must have seen me. I'm not sure why, but it seemed to matter.

Looking back, I've been down the sidewalk a hundred times. I knew that there were spots that were uneven. I knew that I should have been more careful. I knew that I should have taken my time to navigate this unwieldy urban terrain. I should have treated it with more respect, because my expectations that everything would be fine proved to be short-sighted.

This could be the case in so many parts of our lives, as our expectations become assumptions.

We all go through this world expecting something. These expectations become our sidewalk. How many of us have expectations that have been pressed upon us by our friends and family? Have you discussed these expectations? In the end, you'll find these expectations are unachievable or not easily understood. When you understand what your expectation is, you'll soon learn what is really possible.

> What if we didn't create a blind spot for others to stand in?

For example, if your expectation of your family is for everyone to be at a certain place at a certain time, then you'll need to discuss these expectations. The other option is to revisit these expectations.

What if we didn't create a blind spot for others to stand in? How could that happen? Maybe there are both appropriate and inappropriate expectations. Maybe we need to have spoken and unspoken expectations. Maybe there are times when we need to revisit or redefine expectations.

Do you have expectations for your significant other? Is he or she aware of those expectations?

I'm not sure that I could ever live without my wife. I expect Connie to take care of me when I'm sick. I expect her to do the shopping for groceries. Connie expects me to earn enough for our living. She expects that I'll come home every night and that I have and always will remain faithful. Connie and I have a lot of expectations that have been communicated and are understood.

Expectations with my kids are different. My relationship with them is different; we have a different point of view of each other. They are in training. They watch others and hopefully have learned lessons about how they should expect things from other people. I hope they've learned how to respect others and earn the respect of others. Hopefully, they've watched how their mom and I have treated each other during the good times and the bad. How we've gotten back to solid ground when it seemed to have crumbled beneath our feet. How do we treat each other when the love we have for each other exudes? How have we gotten this far?

My mom and dad had been married 66 years when my dad passed away in April of 2015. They had an expectation that they were one, and that was mutual. Being the youngest of ten kids, I was the last to get married. While two of my brothers had passed away before they were old enough to be married, the rest of my siblings have all been married longer than I have to their first and only spouse. We all had the same expectation.

Expectations can also be the reason for someone's struggles when reality sets in. These expectations might not be easily understood.

I struggled for years after having brain surgery because I expected my vision to return to normal. I expected both of my eyes to become open and to see clearly. Once I realized my new reality, something wonderful happened.

> Once I realized my new reality, something wonderful happened.

I was able to see how much I had been missing. All of a sudden, I realized that it took me going blind in order to see clearly. I'm now able to understand a lot of things that I never could before — like the meaning of grace. It's a gift that has already been given to us by our cre-

> I was able to see how much I had been missing.

ator. It's rather interesting that the one that created us also says, "Yeah, I know you're not perfect and that's OK." We only need to accept grace to receive it whenever and wherever we are. You may be saying, "Wait, how can that be? How can there be

> I realized that it took me going blind in order to see clearly.

a gift waiting for me, if I just receive it?" Well, that's exactly what grace is. We've all been given it, but only a few accept it.

Once I accepted grace, it became clear that I haven't lost nearly as much as I've gained since having brain surgery.

The self-limiting belief that I didn't deserve grace had been holding me back. Now, I'm able to move forward with a newfound mission.

Like me, you'll need to give yourself grace to find a way to work around your shortcomings. I know that I need to stand in a certain position and sit at a certain spot at the table for me to have the best experience. I even like to sit in a certain location during presentations or church service. It's never easy. But, as John F. Kennedy once said, "we choose to go to the moon . . . not because [it's] easy but because [it's] hard." Getting through those difficult times makes us stronger and more able to handle the obstacles that lie ahead.

Giving grace to other people will also be key to getting over those obstacles, and help you see what you might have missed in them.

I can now understand that you can love someone even though you may not like them. This is similar to how you hate the sin and love the sinner. It's not about forgetting or wiping the slate clean, but it is about loving them the same way after the sin as before. They are the same people that you love. It just so happens that they made a decision that maybe you wouldn't have made. It shouldn't change the way that you look at them. You shouldn't define someone for the least of which they did, but by the best of which they did.

Would you want someone to sum up your life by the worst thing that you've ever done? Of course not. So, why should you do the same thing to other people? Let's remove the idea of being judged by the least of which you've done. Leave the past in your past, and resolve to do only good in the future. Sounds easy, right? Well, let's just say that you should strive to make more mature, well-informed decisions in the future. It may not be that easy, but once you've let go of the past, you're going to experience much more than you've ever imagined in the future.

Of all of the terrible things that I've said and done in the past, none of them are keeping me from writing this book to you. Sure, there are many things going through my head telling me that I'm not good enough for this assignment, but I'm not letting that stop me. I will continue on and tell you these things because I want to help you.

Those things that you value and believe the most are what you will be remembered for. Whether you're interested in being remembered that way or you're interested in writing a new chapter for your life, you're right where you need to be — about to read Chapter 3.

CHAPTER 3

QUESTION YOUR BELIEFS — SEE WHAT'S REALLY IMPORTANT TO YOU

I used to think that my life on earth revolved around golf, the Ohio State Buckeyes football team, and the Chicago Cubs. They were all that seemed to matter, and those three things really didn't change very much. My golf game was usually frustrating, but enjoyable. The glimpses of hope that I was improving at it always seemed to bring me back to the course. The Buckeyes seemed to win an awful lot, and the Cubs always seemed to lose an awful lot.

This was how I spent my free time when I wasn't working. It was what really mattered to me. Oh my, how times have changed. All of these things are now secondary to my faith, family, and friendships. These new priorities have true meaning because they have the ability to be with me forever. And, yes, that's a long time.

Golf is a sport where even the elite struggle. They can hit bad shots just like I can. Granted, they don't make nearly as many, but they still have the ability to make an error: hit a bad ball, take a bad bounce, or experience adverse weather. There are so many things that can affect my score, so I have to expect the unexpected. I have to realize that at some point, it's out of my control. I wasn't born with a God-given ability to golf with the professionals and certainly not given the time to hone what little skill I have.

Because my change in vision diminished the enjoyment that I received from golf, I wondered whether there was a reason that I had gone blind. Golf used to be my identity. It was my normal. It was my life. As time progressed, I realized that I received just as much enjoyment from the fellowship as I did the actual golfing. That realization led me to continue with the fellowship, because I didn't need two good eyes for that. Blindness helped me see what mattered.

The things that mean the most to you shouldn't be outside your sphere of influence.

> The things that mean the most to you shouldn't be outside your sphere of influence.

Here's what really matters to me: faith, family, and friendships.

Faith is something that is extremely personal. No matter how hard you might try, you can't give it to someone. You can only try to disciple them by helping them when they have questions. You'll need to lead them when they need led, and shadow them when they need shadowed. Before you can do any of these things, you have to first earn their trust. You have to show them that you're a true friend and that you have their best interest in mind. You need to talk to them and understand them. It's important that you know them before you can know how to help them.

When you go the tailor to get pants hemmed or fitted for a suit, what's the first thing that he does? He measures you. Why? Because it's his way of getting to know you. What if you want to go back to school, and you go in to talk with a guidance counselor, what will the guidance counselor want to do? They're going to want to get to know you. It's your job to let them into your world. They can't help you unless they know you.

I realize that we don't all believe in the same thing. My beliefs may not be your beliefs. You'll need to decide for yourself what path you're going to take. All I can do is help you to understand what I believe and why.

Have you ever questioned your faith? If you're telling the truth, I'm sure that you have. It's not a bad thing to do.

Family is important because they represent who I am. I am the son of Wally and Mary Jo Wagner and the youngest of ten children. We lived on a farm, and living on a farm meant working on a farm — something that rarely put a smile on my face. There were many times that I swore never to become a farmer like my dad.

And yet, I am like my dad. It's been said that I have the Wagner smile. If you knew my dad, you'd know what I mean. When he smiled, his whole face smiled. I mean to tell you it was from ear to ear. There was no mistaking it. Even when you would talk to him on the phone, you could tell whether he was smiling. Admittedly, it was usually a good guess that he was. He always seemed to have the ability to see the positive part of almost anything. I really believe that he never met a stranger, and even those that he didn't know soon became his friends.

I'm also the husband and father of my own family. My hope is that my kids and maybe even their kids will some day read this book and nod in agreement that I was much like my dad in those ways.

Do you have someone in your family or someone who seems like family whom you look up to? Have you told them that? This could be a great conversation starter. If not, do you have a friend who could be considered a family member?

For me, friendships that last are not easy to come by. I've been blessed to have some of the best friends in the world, starting with my friend John whom I've known since he moved to our school district in the first grade. I used to draw pictures of Snoopy that I would give to John, and he would collect them. His mom, Mimsi, would arrange for us to get together and go bowling or ride around on his 3-wheeler as kids.

In February of our fourth-grade year, he was involved in a farming accident. His hand got caught in an auger, and his fingers were severed. He endured several surgeries to reattach them, but they would never be the same. He too had to adjust to a new normal.

Forty some years later, he's still someone that I go to for advice. He's always been someone that I look up to and admire.

My friend John is different than my friend Eric.

I wouldn't dare rate or judge the level of a friendship, but the one that I have with my friend Eric is certainly one that has endured the majority of my adult life. There has never been a time that I've questioned the level of honesty and trust in our friendship. He is the one that I could call in the middle of the night. He's also the one that I could be with and not say a word. Sometimes those are the most gratifying times. We've been around each other long enough to know what the other is thinking. Quiet silence is our way of respecting that understanding.

Eric actually flew from Ohio to Phoenix, Arizona to be with me and Connie (he'll tell you it was mostly Connie) when I had brain surgery. Who does that?

Then there are newer friends, like Ken. He has pushed me to expand beyond the person that I am today and grow into the person that I can be. It can be uncomfortable at times, but that's when you know you're growing. If you don't have those growing pains and the desire to learn new things, I'd say to you what Andy said to Red in *The Shawshank Redemption*:

"I guess it comes down to a simple choice, really. Get busy living or get busy dying."

I don't include my wife in my list of friends, because she's more than a friend; she's part of me and I'm part of her. It may sound corny, but we DO complete each other. It could be said that she is my everything.

When I think of what my friends mean to me, it brings to mind the guides on the floor of the car wash. You know, the ones that you're supposed to keep your tires in. Well, those guides have become problematic for me. With only my left eye open, everything seems to be farther right than what it is. When I'm pulling in the car wash, I'm torn between watching the car wash attendant, who is directing me, and looking down at the guides. It's a nerve-wracking 10 seconds

> Once in the guides, everything becomes a little easier to manage.

that hasn't always ended well. There have been times when I've entered the brushless carwash where there is no attendant, and I'm left on my own. Inevitably, I've run over the guides or left my car in a pinch once I get stopped.

Our friends are like those guides to keep us going straight and moving forward. Once in the guides, everything becomes a little easier to manage. Friends can help make life a little easier through their support and advisement.

If you're not sure, here's how to tell what your "everything" is:

Where do you spend most of your time?

Where do you spend most of your money?

If I were to meet someone close to you, let's say your spouse, how would they introduce you?

Answering these questions should clarify what is paramount in your life.

CHAPTER 4

QUESTION YOUR ASSUMPTIONS — SEE YOUR TRAITS TO TREASURE

One day, while I was working at IBM, I asked my boss about some organizational changes that were taking place. Being the newer kid on the block, I asked whether there was someone or a committee of people that had a vision for where all of this movement would be taking the company. I figured that certainly with 350,000 employees, there must be someone with a "crystal ball" who could see where the market was turning, and that our goal was to be out in front.

His response was a little unnerving. Without hesitation, he said, "No, there really isn't a vision. We're simply trying to react to the market."

It made sense that if there were someone with a longer-term vision guiding us, we would be able to move more quickly, if we started sooner. It seemed logical that with a company of our depth and breadth, there had to be a driving factor behind such serious actions. If you've never been at a large company, I can tell you that there are times that logic takes a back seat. There are times that whatever seems valuable to you isn't valued by the company. That what seems to be logical for your customer is not logical in the eyes of your leader.

I've had the chance to meet with some of these leaders. Some real "big deals" who hardly had time for little guys like me. They could sometimes look right through me and seem to be thinking of the answer to my question, even before I asked it. They were blind to the customer issues I saw as something we needed to address.

Companies like Sears, hhgregg, Payless, and RadioShack weren't as lucky as IBM. They have shrunk to a fraction of what they once were. Companies like Amazon have changed the retail model for this market segment, because they saw where the market was headed.

There were a number of contributing factors to the downfall of RadioShack, but *Fortune* magazine summarizes the evolution of the industry and their inability to react as one of the more substantial factors[1]. This can be attributed to a multitude of circumstances, not the least of which was the economy. However, many of RadioShack's competitors seemed to weather the storm.

It seems as though my life was on a trajectory similar to RadioShack's in 2010 and 2011. But, I had the "good fortune" of going blind, which made me question my assumptions. After that, I didn't take nearly as much for granted. I was seemingly able to "see" so much better than I ever had.

Losing a good deal of my eyesight and not knowing when or if I'd ever get it back was one of the hardest things

---

[1] (*Fortune* magazine http://fortune.com/2017/03/07/radioshack-bankrupt-again/)

that I'd ever had to deal with. Believe it or not, it's actually turned out to be one of the best things that could have happened to me. My life is forever changed.

At the age of 43, after having brain surgery and not being able to see, I actually found something that I didn't know was missing. Obviously it wasn't something that I expected to find. What I found was one of those "traits to treasure." As the author of *Ordinary Superpowers*, Mark Henson, would say, I discovered one of my ordinary superpowers: steadfast optimism.

A good friend of mine once told me how much he admired me for having such a positive attitude. He was genuine when he asked how I remained so positive. He, like many other people, asked, "how do you do it?"

The fact of the matter is I get this trait from my dad. Part of that is credited to him being a farmer. I eluded the farming profession, but not the positive attitude that he had. This is where it all starts and ends for me. From the time that I wake up until the time that I lay my head on the pillow, being positive is something that I'll always do. Even when I was blind, I had to use positive words; I had to use positive thoughts. I had to use positive energy to combat so many negative ones that were surrounding me.

Many people in a situation like mine would just as soon stay in the house and live a meager, if not hermit-like, existence. When the time came for pictures to be taken or the front doorbell rang, they would suddenly become transparent.

A friend of the family once interviewed my mom and dad, and asked them how they managed to persevere after they lost two of their sons on separate occasions. There was never a question for them. They just continued on with eight other hungry mouths to feed. My dad worked from sunup to sundown and many hours beyond to provide for us. He would often tell us, "You don't know how lucky you are." He was right. We were spoiled. Spoiled because of his hard work. Because of his successful business. Because of the way he formed and kept honest relationships. Our parents set a wonderful example for all of us to follow — an example of remaining positive during difficult circumstances.

As my dad farmed, it must have been awful to pass by where my brother Mike was killed in a farming accident, or for him or my mom to go by where my brother Ray was killed in an automobile accident.

How do you take that same positive attitude, drive, and initiative, and give it to the next generation or to others around you? How do you instill in them the same drive and initiative that we keep the business growing?

It has to be more than a "carrot and stick" approach. Whether it's true or not isn't clear, but this is an adage for how our ancestors used to get their mules to do what they wanted them to do. You see, they could entice them by hanging a carrot just out of reach of their mouth. This would be something that the mule would try and get to, causing him to move forward in quest of the carrot. The "stick" reference is that they would make a switch or whip out of a stick. With the stick, they would punish the mule when it didn't do as they wanted. It was assumed that one of these two methods would work.

What assumptions are you making about yourself that should be questioned? Are you assuming that you're better than you thought in certain areas? Any time that you're in a dark place or not sure which way that you should turn, you should identify what traits you're good at, and begin to emphasize those that you can begin to develop. If that's still unclear, it may be helpful to go through a self-assessment, such as the StrengthsFinder® test found at: http://www.strengthstest.com/

There are many times in my life that I needed someone to tell me that I am better than even I thought I was, someone like Barnabas in the Bible. He was a true encourager. Those are times when I'm vulnerable and wondering whether I've made the best choices in life. These people come around me and without prompting, fill me up with all of the good work that I've done. Not because they want to give me false hope, but because they truly value me and the work that I've done. They don't want to see everything that I've done go to waste. This is a remarkable trait in someone, and I would encourage you to be one of those people for someone else. You can't expect someone to be that person for you until you've filled that role for someone else. Help others find their traits to treasure, and they will help you find yours too.

During my working career, I've experienced all sorts of personalities, good and bad. There was the "type A" personality who always acted like he was behind no matter how far ahead he was. There was the reluctant hero who just seemed to be in the right place at the right time. Then there was the party boy who worked hard all day so he could party hard all night. In some cases, I've possessed those personalities. If I can leave you with one thing from this chapter, I want you to know that you are not defined by the worst things that you've done, whether they're personal or professional. You will be measured by your consistency in striving for growth.

There are so many things that we could view as obstacles, but can also be seen as opportunities for growth.

There's an old story of a frog that fell into a bucket of milk. He kicked and kicked and kicked. There was no way that he was ever going to get out. But then, as he continued to kick, he realized that milk was slowly turning into a more solid form. Eventually it turned into butter, and the frog was able to climb out. Not only did he get out, but he was also much stronger after kicking all that time.

> There are so many things that we could view as obstacles, but can also be seen as opportunities for growth.

At first, he probably thought that it was an obstacle. In the end, it became an opportunity to grow.

STEP 2

SIGHT — VIEW YOUR
HIDDEN TREASURE

TREASURES EXIST IN OUR TIME AND TALENT

CHAPTER 5

IDENTIFY YOUR OBSTACLES — VIEW WHAT'S HARD TO SEE

When I was 10 years old, I started to learn that there were things that I'd never be able to do. This is when I began to notice some of the issues that I was born with that can't be seen. It's when I had my first shunt put in. When I first saw double for a brief period of time. The first time that I was involuntarily unconscious. Looking back, that seems to be a very early age to have limitations put on you. Especially for a young boy who loved to do anything that involved a ball, it was heartbreaking.

I never cared much for work on the farm, but I loved sports. It was what I could always be a part of, even after that summer when I started experiencing my limitations. It didn't matter that I wasn't the best one of the team, it mattered that I was *on* the team. It mattered that it was something that was a constant source of FUN. It mattered that people actually were cheering for me and wanted me to do well. This is something I miss from my childhood. I can't blame it on anyone or anything; maybe it's just a part of growing up. Maybe it's part of being the youngest of 10 kids. Maybe it's my belief that I was created for a different reason.

Knowing that people are cheering for me is important. That's one of the reasons that this has been so hard. I want people to understand that what I go through every day is difficult, but at the same time I don't want them to have pity on me. I want them to treat me like anyone else. I don't want any special favors.

Unfortunately there for a while, I had to be treated differently. In the first few days after having brain surgery, Connie and I would walk around the block that our hotel sat on. It would take many more months for my left eye to begin to open, and my right eye never did, so these walks meant Connie was holding onto my arm and leading the way.

I wasn't aware of any of my obstacles until it was too late. That's exactly what happened as we were taking one of our strolls on the sidewalk. As we slowly went along, all of a sudden, OUCH! Connie had taken her eye off of me, and I walked directly into a cactus! While it wasn't amusing at the time, we've laughed about it a lot since then. If I'd have had S.I.G.H.T., I could have avoided this obstacle... and some painful needles.

Maybe this tool can help you going forward.

Self-inspection — As we are beginning to become more familiar with the world around us, we also become more familiar with ourselves. We begin to understand our strengths and limitations for what they are. Not that we're able to do anything with them yet, but still, recognizing them is the first step.

We all need to have a long look in the mirror on a regular basis. It's important to write down our goals and dreams. Once we've done that, we need to understand what's keeping us from them. Is it something that we have the power to change? If it is, how can we change it? Will we need help?

Increasing — We all must increase our self-worth and improve for our own good and for the good of others if we want to see the world that we live in improve too. It's even more important for us to help to share our long-term goal with others as they go through life along side you. There is a real need to allow our peers to see that goal so they can encourage us to reach it.

Peers don't have to be friends. Maybe they're just acquaintances that seem to want to help. These peers are usually people with similar thoughts but different ideas. These people are crucial for the success of your organization or your personal goals.

Gaining — This is a race to the finish, but it's not always a race that was meant to be won. We are raised with the understanding that it's always about who gets to the goal first. Some people say, "The early bird gets the worm." It may be true that the early bird gets *a* worm, but who says that there's only one? We need to focus on our own goals and not be as concerned with those around us, at the same time keeping a positive attitude about a plentiful life.

Healing — There is only one way to achieve true healing; it occurs from the inside out. When we discussed how we all have one creator in common, it's also true that this is where our healing comes from. Spiritual healing is long-lasting healing. From a worldly perspective, healing should still be taken to a higher level than ourselves. It could mean going to your doctor, psychiatrist, coach, banker, pastor/priest, or someone else. It needs to be an expert in the actual field or a related field. This will allow someone that you may not know as well to give you some tough advice to help you heal.

Teaching — To have the opportunity to speak with others regarding the trouble spots that they've encountered is always satisfying. It's satisfying not because they are struggling, but because talking about those things is therapy. It allows them to let others know of their plight. It gives them a feeling that someone else will carry their burdens for a little while, even if that's not exactly what's happening.

Now that we've discovered what our "everything" is and where our "blind spots" are, we can talk about the obstacles to get to our goal.

Use S.I.G.H.T. as a tool for obstacle identification.

In the business world, there are many different obstacles. One intent of this book is to discuss the employee obstacles — which, in turn, are inherently employer obstacles.

Even if you don't have obstacles today, you should be practicing how to overcome issues in the future. Practice, practice, practice.

Listen. Take notes. Listen some more.

Don't be afraid to ask yourself hard questions.

Now that you're identifying the obstacles in life, you can view what your necessities are.

CHAPTER 6

IDENTIFY YOUR NECESSITIES — VIEW THE NECESSARY EVIL

I am in need.

Although she usually took me where I needed to go, there were a few times that Connie couldn't give me a ride. The first time that happened, I had a meeting in downtown Columbus. It was beautiful summer day.

My colleague Eric volunteered to drop me off on his way to another meeting. When I got out of the car, he asked me if I would be okay. "Sure," I said, "of course." I was scared as hell, but I refused to let on to anyone that this was the case. So, I just started walking. I've come to realize that most people don't realize that my eyesight is greatly diminished. I guess I act as though there's nothing wrong at all, but if they could only see what I see, then they'd understand that this isn't easy. They'd begin to understand that the guy behind those weakened lids is struggling. He's struggling to string together steps without falling. He's struggling to put together sentences while understanding that the other person is still listening. He's struggling to be comfortable in his own skin.

With my final destination in mind, I started my journey. I didn't really know where I was, and I certainly didn't know how to get there. On top of all of that, I was walking along the wide Columbus city sidewalks with one hand holding one of my eyelids open. It makes things interesting when your two eyeballs don't go together. The light that my eyes have coming into them is greatly reduced, and when I am able to see out of both eyes, everything is double.

I've never been a "why me?" kind of guy, but it does make a person wonder.

As I walked down the sidewalk of downtown Columbus, I noticed that I was passing by a bus stop, not unlike any other bus stop where there are people from all walks of life. I realized that I'm just one of them. I feel like one of God's misfit toys, like I belong somewhere that I've never fit in before. One of these days I'll stop with the stereotypes and appreciate people for who they are. They're people with stories. We all have them. Do they know mine? No. Do I know theirs? No. Why, then, do I give them one without asking?

Thankfully, the sidewalk was even, and there were no corners sticking up or holes for me to step in. You know, the ones that take your breath away when there's an extra drop that you weren't expecting. Or the spots that trip you up and make you look like you're drunk or something. It's those moments that make you feel like you're an outcast, when you're probably like a lot of other people. I'm sure that many people take a stumble over the course of the day.

Why then do we have to personalize it? I'm willing to bet you that there are people with similar issues to yours, you just don't see it. I'm willing to bet you that there are people that are stumbling over the same metaphorical edge of cement, you just don't know it. Remember that you're not alone. No matter where you go or what you do, we all have something in common. It's the common bond that makes us stronger. It's the bond that helps us to understand that it's going to be okay. It's the bond that drives us to tell others and to help them to understand the same thing.

Our common bond is our creator.

I kept walking and kept thinking of how scared I was, but I kept going. Connie was always only a phone call away, but I knew that neither one of us needed that.

Finally, I reached my destination — I thought.

Unfortunately, I walked into the wrong establishment. It was the Subway restaurant next door to the restaurant where we were meeting. When you can only use one eye, and even that one doesn't see peripherally, you sometimes miss things. I'm sure that I've missed many handshakes, glances at pretty girls, and views of wild socks with fine shoes. But, in this instance I was only one door away. I was actually headed to one of Columbus' old-style restaurants, The Elevator. Interesting how I was certain that I was headed for The Elevator and ended up in the Subway. One has the ability to take you up, and the other requires you to go down.

I ended up finding my way to the correct restaurant and was shown to the correct table. The meeting was fruitful and, when it was over, one of the other attendees took me home.

It's the uneven parts of the sidewalk and the cracks in the concrete that are the necessary evil. They are there to remind us that we're not going to able to just walk down the sidewalk without a care in the world. We weren't put on this earth to have a simple and robotic life. We're going to have to pick our head up from time to time in order to see the goal or at least the next milestone. Even by doing that, there will still be times that the height of the sidewalk changes. Peaks and valleys will sometimes be hidden. For me, since I don't have three-dimensional vision, they'll always be hidden.

How do you identify your necessities in life?

- Do you need to make more money?
- How do you distinguish between wants and needs?
- What do you really need out of life?

We complicate our lives because we want too many things. If we were to simplify our wants to our necessities, our life would be much different forever.

Winston Churchill once said, "A pessimist sees the difficulty in every opportunity; an optimist see the opportunity in every difficulty."

CHAPTER 7

IDENTIFY YOUR MOMENT —
VIEW THE TRIGGER EVENT

There is no way to foretell what will happen later in life. If you take inventory of these significant moments as you go through life, you'll have a better understanding of where these moments are leading. Picture this.

You're sitting in your lifeboat without a care in the world, and you seemingly run ashore onto a R.E.E.F. What do you do? Wait a minute, what's a R.E.E.F.? In this case, a R.E.E.F. is an obstacle that keeps you from moving forward. It can sometimes be moved, and it can always be navigated. Regardless of whether you go around it, over it, or just point your boat in a different direction.

A R.E.E.F. is one of those moments in life that include one or more of the following:

- **R**elationship problems
- **E**thical issues
- **E**motional distress
- **F**inancial burdens

We all encounter these moments throughout the course of our days. However, we don't always identify them as the issue that they are.

Relationship problems are not limited to your significant other. They can be with a coworker, sibling, or child. Since the time of my surgery, I believe I've gotten clearer with my relationships. That doesn't mean that I've written anyone off, and it doesn't mean that I like everyone.

It does mean that I try to *love* everyone. Some days, that can be difficult. You may be wondering how you can love someone without liking them. There are plenty of people who don't do things the way that I do. For example, there's a couple at one of the churches we used to attend. They have always been very involved and have been servant leaders all along the way. They're nice people and I love them, but they do things differently than I would.

At the same time, there are people that I have a great affinity for. These people are some of my closest friends. I like these people, because among other reasons, they're more like me. I can relate to them.

Take Bob. He was a good friend and someone who I could bounce ideas off of. We were so similar. We were about the same age, worked in the same profession and even at the same company, we both had kids that were similar ages, we were both men of faith and never seemed too interested in changing much in our lives.

My relationship with Bob was great, and then it came time for me to leave the company. I was pursuing a job that paid more money, and I thought that this was the way to do it. It was a difficult transition to say the least, and I soon felt that I had left for the wrong reason. But after a year, I was feeling confident in my surroundings and was even put into a management role.

When I had a spot on my team that needed to be filled, Bob was the first one I called. We worked out the agreement, and he started soon thereafter. It was great to have him on the team, but I had no idea what was coming next.

I placed Bob at a customer site, and he was not happy. I told him that when the current customer agreement had expired, we would bring him back to the office and find another role. In the meantime, a number of things changed, and I had to go back on my word. He was furious and ended up leaving the company. After that day, I didn't talk to Bob for more than 10 years, and then, one Christmas season, I ran into him in the mall. I told him that I was sorry and asked for his forgiveness.

He showed me the proper way of handling our relationship. It was as if he didn't even remember that there was any contention between us. He had forgiven me long before I had forgiven myself. It was a true lesson for me that day. It had kept me from thinking that I should ever be a manager again. It seemed like I had sold him out and would crumble, when in a similar situation, again.

Holding on to animosity or guilt will prevent you from holding on to any relationship. Releasing others from those feelings will set you free and allow you the spiritual peace that makes for fertile ground where seeds of long-standing relationships can grow.

Ethical issues are always something that we struggle with, for the simple reason that it can be hard to know where you draw the line. It seems like a "cut and dry" issue, but let me put this in context.

One of the best ways to determine whether you're handling a situation ethically is whether you have to ask yourself or someone else, "Am I handling this situation ethically?" It's not often that you'll ask yourself that question when you're already deep in the thick of it. However, there may still be time to correct your course. This is where you need to seek out advice and counsel from mentors and coaches that know you and whom you know to have a strong sense of ethics.

Try not to dismiss them and think, "Well, this is a unique situation and I'm sure that they wouldn't understand. It'll take too long to explain it to them." Those are excuses for not doing the due diligence that will help you. It's important that you follow through with this counsel to ensure that you continue to walk the appropriate path.

I'm sure that there are examples of events that I've handled unethically. It's difficult to recall any because they've been sealed away in my memory or they've been "justified" for some mysterious reasons that may or may not be appropriate. They are certainly out there for all of us, it's only a matter of understanding that when they arise in the future, we need to deal with them head-on. We need to take the time to ensure that they don't happen again. Like my relationship with Bob, it will keep you from moving forward. You'll be judging YOURSELF by the least of things that you have done.

Emotional distress may seem like something that doesn't affect you, but when the chips are down, it could become readily apparent and, by then, it's too late.

In one sales job I had, things were going great — I was doing what I was supposed to be doing, and achieving the numbers that I was supposed to achieve. Then one day, out of the blue, it seemed my management team must have decided that it was time to "turn the screws." That meant that they were pushing another agenda without allowing me the proper time to prepare.

Within weeks, they initiated a Quarterly Business Review (QBR), which was well within their right. They began the review by asking for additional information above what I'd ever been accustomed to and then, when they didn't get it, they put me in a conference room and began to interrogate me. While I was sitting in my chair, at the large conference table, they placed themselves in front of me with the table behind them, leaving almost no space between us. They began to question my integrity and my commitment to the job. "Perhaps your speaking and writing is getting in the way." "Perhaps you should regain your focus."

When I left that meeting, I was a mess. I called Connie but didn't reach her, so I left her a voicemail. While I was explaining to her how my QBR went, I just broke down. That was the first time that this job had ever gotten to me that much. I was having a tough time with how things were being handled, and I couldn't hide it from my wife. It was something that I had never expected, and I was certain something like that could never happen to me, but it did. It paralyzed me and kept me from seeing a future with that company. I couldn't see a way forward.

Then there are times that emotional distress is raw and on the surface. The death of a loved one comes to mind. Recently, my dad passed away after he was diagnosed with kidney failure following a bout with gout. It was a six-month process that didn't end the way that anyone wanted it to. He was the cornerstone of our family and always will be. It was difficult to let him go, but we all have fond memories from his life. Six months later, my mother-in-law was diagnosed with pneumonia, and within a week had breathed her last breath.

Both of these instances were difficult to deal with, and both carried heavy emotional distress. We dealt with both of them in the best possible way that we could. No one should ever have to go through that, but we all will. Even though we were struggling with two big losses, we still had to take care of our kids.

Be inspired to find something that you'll always want to live for. What gives you the most joy? What "fills your tank"? This will be what you want to remember when you encounter your own R.E.E.F.

> What "fills your tank"? This will be what you want to remember when you encounter your own R.E.E.F.

Financial concerns are something that we all experience at some point in our life. It's certainly not something that I'm immune to, and I realize that managing money is not my strong suit. So, what are you supposed to do if you're not good with money? I seek the advice of people that I recognize as smarter than I am in financial matters. Although they may not look like it, most people have financial concerns — whether it's managing money in general, saving for retirement, or paying for college. This is when you need to build your network of friends, and within your current network you should be looking for those individuals that are better than you.

There are a few options, but none that have been recommended to me as much as *Financial Peace University* by Dave Ramsey. There is a way out of debt. The bigger secret is how to never get in debt. Financial Peace University can help you with both.

Living within your means sounds easier than it really is. I wish I had listened to someone when I was younger. You don't have to make the same mistakes that I made.

Feeling good for the moment can make you feel dirty for a lifetime.

So, when you hit a R.E.E.F., should you go back to one of these remedies? Sure, but it would be better if you started to prepare yourself for the inevitable now. This reminds me of the story about the young man who asked his landscaper the best way to get a big oak tree to grow in his yard. You see, the young man was impatient and willing to pay extra for a full-sized tree. When the landscaper heard the question, he thought about it and politely said, "Plant it 20 years ago."

You may not find that funny when you're trying to smooth things out on a rocky road, but I hope that it encourages you to start looking into these things now.

CHAPTER 8

IDENTIFY YOUR MASTERY —
VIEW A NEW WORLD

We all have hardships in life. At some point, we all struggle with something.

For me, that summer day in 2011, my hardship was literally going blind. When I finally had sight again, I was able to make it out into the world unsupervised. Then, I got to experience many more obstacles as I walked down that sidewalk in downtown Columbus.

Before, I wouldn't have ever experienced those obstacles, because someone would have dropped me off right at the door of my final destination. Now that I have sight, there's a new set of hurdles to overcome. I think that's how life is. It's like your first day at school when you're in kindergarten. Once you finally are comfortable and in your zone at elementary school, they move you to middle school. Each time, you're starting over. Then you're a freshman, four years of high school, and if you go to college, you're a freshman again. I'm not sure about you, but I've never felt very refreshed about being called a freshman again. In life, it's the same way. Once you gain knowledge and are competent, you have the chance to expand that knowledge and grow more competent. Going through life is a never-ending learning process. Along with growing up and dealing with obstacles, our school years establish a base for future learning.

That sidewalk I've mentioned in previous chapters had all of the obstacles that I could handle that hot summer day. But, that was what I had set my mind on doing. I didn't overthink it; I just did it. It seemed unfortunate that my driver couldn't drop me off at the door. Looking back, it was probably a good thing that I had to walk a block or two.

As I walked along, thoughts of something bad happening began to enter my mind. I could see people moving around me. It was a good thing that they could see me, because I couldn't see them. What if one of them took advantage of my situation? What if they knocked me down, grabbed my wallet, or something worse? If something did happen, what would Connie say? She's always trying to break my fall. What she doesn't realize is that I *need* to fall; it's only then that I'll understand how far I can go. That's how we know that we're alive. It's when we do new things. Sometimes we succeed, and sometimes we fail. When we fail, we learn a lot more than when we succeed.

> Sometimes we succeed, and sometimes we fail. When we fail, we learn a lot more than when we succeed.

So, I continued my walk. Which, to be honest, is more of a stumble even when I've had plenty of coffee.

I guess that could be another obstacle that we need to overcome. How do we fulfill the purpose that God has given us and continue to be a good spouse, parent, sibling, or offspring? That's what they refer to as "work-family life balance." It's a term that's been around for years, and it's meant to make you stop and consider how your actions, whether they are for your business or for your family, are impacting the other half of the equation. This assumes that there are only two variables in the equation. In addition, there is the belief that our work should not define us.

What that concept doesn't take into consideration is the spiritual side of the equation. Most people would think that this value goes into the family category. Is that true? When you're running kids or loved ones to these spiritual activities, then yes. However, when you are investing in the spiritual side of yourself, that's a whole 'nother story.

When you make investments in the spiritual side, you begin to invest in YOU. This is not specific to the home-and-family YOU. This is not specific to the business leader and cog-in-the-wheel YOU, even if you serve in the ministry.

The spiritual side of our lives doesn't belong in either "bucket." Your beliefs are something that you can't give to someone else or command them to believe in. At the same time, the spiritual side is very real, and it needs to be considered for its own merits. Spirituality takes a person from being an important contributor at work and in society to being a true leader. A leader for his work. A leader for his family. A leader for his community. A leader for life.

Balance is another obstacle that I encountered on this sidewalk. There are times when I'm moving along just as I'm supposed to, and then there are times that the sidewalk is a tad bit uneven, and that's enough to cause me to stumble.

Going faster makes it easier for me to keep my balance and appear as though I don't have other issues, but what if I'm going in the wrong direction? That means I'll be able to realize my mistake sooner. Is that a good thing? I'd rather go to the correct place the first time. How do I ensure that I'm going to the right place?

Having work-life balance is one thing, but having internal balance is quite another. It's the physical and spiritual battle that we all fight. Am I eating the right things? Am I exercising enough? Do I drink the right things? Do I have a good set of core abdominal muscles? Do I exercise my brain by reading and learning? Do I fill my tank with the right things in life? The more that you fill your tank with the right things, the less room there is for the wrong things.

Obstacles in your life will lead you to question right from wrong. They will make you sidestep a dangerous situation. Obstacles will allow you to experience all that life has to give. But, more than any of those things, obstacles will

> Obstacles will force you to grow.

force you to grow. They will force you to get out of your comfort zone. When you do, your comfort zone changes, and then the next experience is bigger and better. They are absolutely a necessity for your growth at work, home, and spiritually. Obstacles are put in place for that reason.

Some of our hurdles in life are put there on purpose to help us learn. You see, it's during times of adversity or failure that you learn the most. It helps to view the world through new eyes.

The way that my dad lived his life was remarkable. It reminds me of a quote.

"A master in the art of living draws no sharp distinction between his work and his play; his labor and his leisure, his mind and his body; his education and his recreation. He hardly knows which is which. He simply pursues his vision of excellence through whatever he is doing and leaves others to determine whether he is working or playing. To himself, he always appears to be doing both."

— *L.P. Jacks*

LIFE BEGINS WHEN ABUNDANCE IS IRRELEVANT

CHAPTER 9

CHART YOUR RESPONSE —
ENVISION YOUR CONTROL

S hould I stay or should I go?
There were many chances, that day of my meeting in downtown Columbus, for me to turn around. The first step was for me to get out of bed, knowing that Connie wouldn't be there. That alone would've been enough to stop me.

Curling up in a ball and hiding from the world seemed like a good idea. But, we all need to, sooner or later, get out of B.E.D. This sort of B.E.D. is an acronym for Blame, Excuse, and Denial. These are three things that keep us from reaching our full potential.

"I'm sorry but I can't make the meeting because the person that knows me best isn't available to drive me there." Like that, I could just **blame** it on someone else. It's her fault, not mine. That's not the right way, but it's the easy way.

"I would have been here on time, but I walked into the wrong building and wasn't comfortable asking for directions." Or, "there were too many uneven parts of the sidewalk and I didn't want to go any further for fear of falling." **Excuses** roll off our tongue without us even thinking.

Denying would mean indicating that there really isn't a problem. In this case, that would be hard to assert. However, I could have denied that there was a meeting or that I had the right time. That would have been denying the real reason for me not attending the meeting — my lack of vision.

We all get stuck in this B.E.D. from time to time. It's important that we draw awareness to it and begin to understand that this is something that happens. Once we do that, we can begin to deal with it.

One of the best ways of dealing with it is to pull out an O.A.R. and start rowing. Not a physical oar, but the O.A.R. that stands for Ownership, Accountability, and Responsibility. Yes, another acronym.

Ownership happens when you get out of B.E.D. That's when you have the ability to redeem the day for its own use. Not for what could have been if you had chosen a different path. Ownership is what brings about a great sense of maturity, and it doesn't come easy to many of us.

Taking ownership means stepping up and owning the current circumstances, regardless of whether they're good or bad. This allows you to operate with a clear conscience and builds your credibility in the world around you.

Accountability to me is the next step in the evolution of maturity. It's one thing to take ownership of the good or the bad. It's quite another thing to stand tall and to be held accountable. This is when we separate the intenders from the pretenders. It reminds me of being in IT Sales.

There are many times that you are not given the opportunity to defend your results, and that QBR meeting was one of them.

Even though I had enjoyed some success, it wasn't enough. Has that ever happened to you? Where you work tirelessly for months and even years on end, but at the end of that time, it doesn't matter how many people liked working with you. It doesn't matter how good your customer relationships are. In the end, it's a numbers game. You simply have to have the numbers to be sustainable in sales.

Responsibility is the outcome of Ownership and Accountability. If you take ownership and you're held accountable, by definition you are responsible. It's rare that you could be responsible without the other two.

Now you're ready to start building on the O.A.R., so the next time that you hit a R.E.E.F., you may not be stuck for as long. This is similar to a bodybuilder who builds muscle only after it has been torn. It has to go through a destructive process in order to become stronger. When thinking of vision for your life, put it in this context, where you use a different lens than the one that you have today.

> Once you have a different lens, your vision will change.

Once you have a different lens, your vision will change. You can think of V.I.S.I.O.N. in this way to serve as a useful tool.

View the world as if you're a child that has just began to walk and talk. You've not heard anyone tell you that you're not smart enough, rich enough, or pretty enough. Clear out those voices from your head, and look into a new mirror. Go blind and look again with your heart.

You'll see what others really see. You'll see someone who's got what it takes to achieve their dreams. You'll see someone who's been waiting to be announced for a long time. You'll see someone who is happy in their own skin.

Inspirational is what you'll be to someone else. While you've spent all of these years looking up to others wondering if you could ever be like them, now you are. You've got something that others aspire to. They've seen where you've come from, but may not understand how you've gotten there, but it will be awesome for you to tell your story as you serve as an inspiration for others. You have just given yourself the responsibility to walk a little taller and talk a little prouder.

Stories about your own journey are important, but so are the stories of others that you've brought along on the journey. The stories of those that have made your journey possible. It's always more fun to talk about the journey than it is to talk about the goal. Ask any Olympic athlete or celebrity about their success, and they will tell you about the people who made their journey possible and the obstacles that they were able to overcome because of those people. They'll tell you stories that don't include standing on the awards podium.

Interest in the banking sense is something that you collect or gain for your money that has been deposited. The idea is that your money can then be used by other people for their benefit. That's not the kind of interest that we're talking about. We aren't interested in having someone reaping the benefit of implementing your treasures and ideas. This is the interest that you'll gain from others as you begin to implement your ideas. Doing these things will allow you to experience the fullness and richness of your own self-worth.

Optimism is a character trait that is a requirement for anyone to have a positive attitude. These are characteristics that can keep you sane and grounded in a turbulent world. It's when Optimism's evil twin Pessimism creeps into your thought process that you leave yourself open to self-doubt and self-destruction. This doesn't mean that we will always be optimistic. It doesn't mean that pessimism is always a bad thing. Having the character trait of optimism simply means that, for the most part, we approach life with an optimistic attitude. This is something that we all get to choose.

> Having the character trait of optimism simply means that, for the most part, we approach life with an optimistic attitude.

Nice people are generally happy people. What kind of effort does it take to be nice? Not much, but here's what you can do when you're faced with a situation. Think of this simple formula:

$$E + R = O$$

It stands for *Event* plus your *Response* equals the *Outcome*. You can learn more about it in Urban Meyer's book, *Above the Line*.

This is what is taught in the R-factor. This comes from Tim Kight, CEO of Focus3, a consulting company that focuses on helping organizations align the power of leaders, culture, and behavior to achieve results. There are books that are committed to this process. It is simple, but like anything, it takes deliberate repetitive intention to make it permanent. However, this will represent HOW you are remembered. As far as WHAT you are remembered for, that's another story.

Do you want to be remembered for a product or service? Maybe you want to be remembered for your community impact or involvement. No matter what it is, if you're going to achieve your goals, you'll have to have a strong core and connection.

In 2012, my good friend Bill Brown suggested that I consider reading a book that was written by a former pastor of his church. He said that it was a book for people that had been through a lot, and it might be helpful for me. Not knowing what he was talking about, I wrote down the name of the book and tucked it away in my memory. Not being a reader, I later dismissed this idea, since it would surely never happen.

Months went by and, as I was talking with another good friend, Rye D'Orazio, lo and behold he brings up the same book and tells me about a monthly meeting that the writer has been holding. It's the second Friday of the month, and I made a point to attend.

It was April of 2013, a little more than two years from the day that I had brain surgery, when I met someone who challenged me. Trust me, I didn't think that I needed to challenged, but he did it anyway. It was the former pastor, a man named Kary Oberbrunner, or as he says, "a bald guy with a girl's name." He and David Branderhorst, his business partner, have become friends, mentors, and coaches of mine and helped me start a new career. These newly formed relationships opened a whole new world of people that poured into me, and I soaked it up.

Like walking down that long sidewalk in downtown Columbus, I eventually got to my destination. I eventually realized some success for my efforts. I eventually got to the point.

That's what you can do too. You can understand the purpose for your life. You can enjoy some success. You can get to the point. It's important to realize that it's not about living to fulfill someone else's goals, someone else's aspirations, or someone else's vision. This is a time when you come first. You have earned the right to say, "it's time for me now."

Stop what you're doing right now. Put down this book and say it: "It's time for me now."

Take 5 minutes and quietly reflect on what you've read so far and think about what it means for this to be about you. Think of the impact you will be able to have on others. Think of your family. They may not recognize you after this. You will be changed forever. After this, when you enter a room, I'm willing to bet you'll hear those magic words, "I want some of what they've got."

> What matters the most is what you put into your mind. What are you looking at? That goes for reading, television, movies, news, social media, websites, and more. What are you listening to? That goes for music, podcasts, and people that you associate with.

What "they've got" is a strong core. A strong belief system. A strong worldview.

This is when you'll start to put together a V.I.S.I.O.N. The way that you come about, putting this together, may be similar to the way that I did. To make it easier to remember, I put it together as follows.

This is one long and winding road that starts with what goes into your mind. What goes into your mind will determine your thoughts, and your thoughts will determine your beliefs. Your beliefs determine the words that you use. These words have a direct correlation with your actions. These actions represent your beliefs and worldview. What matters the most is what you put into your mind. What are you looking at? That goes for reading, television, movies, news, social media, websites, and more. What are you listening to? That goes for music, podcasts, and people that you associate with.

What you think would be a simple question really isn't. What do you believe in?

Take this time to write out 20 statements for what you believe. We'll revisit them in Chapter 11, and you can also look at mine. As you write these statements, think of where you spend your time. Where do you spend your thoughts? Where do you spend your money?

CHAPTER 10

CHART YOUR DREAMS —
ENVISION YOUR DESTINY

"The World May Be Broken But Hope Is Not Crazy"
— John Green

D o you have a dream for your life?
Once you become an adult and start your first job, your dreams seem to take a back seat. You settle down and get into the groove of performing the work that you were trained to do. Your life changes from planning, training, and hoping to just doing. You get comfortable in the daily duty. Maybe you love the daily duty at first, until it turns into the daily grind. The kind of grind that makes you hate Mondays and worship Fridays. Then, sooner or later, that grind turns into a rut.

A *rut* as defined in the dictionary as "a long deep track made by the repeated passage of the wheels of vehicles." This passage is you going back and forth to work every day and running the same errands every weekend. That means that your rut will prevent you from venturing off the track that you've been traveling. Some people may enjoy this, but I'm guessing that you're not one of them.

I've also heard it referred to as a grave with the ends open.

I used to be a person who enjoyed the rut, because it was common and consistent. I never had to worry about the next paycheck because it was always there — until it wasn't. That's when I had a better appreciation for the rut. It wasn't until I was removed from the rut that I had a better appreciation for what it was. It's not always a bad thing, but it can lead to a place that isn't where you want to be. You see, when you're in a rut and you want to turn one way or the other, you can't. The walls of the rut — that you've built — prevent you from doing anything but going down the same path that you've been traveling.

If you're like me, you stayed in the rut too long and you weren't sure how you could get out. Maybe you didn't know that there was anything else. After spending some time in this place, you became susceptible to a common condition known as a "funk." This is a sad state of depression that can have serious effects on your well-being. If you're finding yourself there, dreaming is one tool that can help you get out.

There are other forms of help, but we need to narrow our focus on getting you out of this rut and funk quickly.

I'm guessing that you dream of getting more out of life. You'd like to experience something different than what you've had for the past few years. I needed help once I got to this realization. Maybe you do too. Here's what it means to dream.

It means imagining that you're in a place different than today. You may have friends or family there with you. Maybe you're celebrating, or just relaxing. You could be at a point where life seems like a vacation. You might not know what everything looks like, but you know how it feels.

Ah, that's it. How does it feel?

The dream has to feel remarkable to change your direction. It has to feel great to create a vision for you. It has to make itself apparent to you in the end.

> The dream has to feel remarkable to change your direction.

There was no point in continuing down that sidewalk in downtown Columbus unless I knew there was something at the end. It had to be something that would allow me to take the next step in my life and career. What would be the point if I were going to a meeting just to sit in the corner and listen to others talk? It had to be intentional.

You also need to be intentional with how you spend your time. The more focused and intentional you are with your dreams, the more likely they are to come true.

> You may have to take imperfect action.

Dreaming can sometimes be a hard thing to do, for most people, for two reasons. One reason is that they're afraid of failure. They've been down this road before. They've sniffed success only to have it pulled away like a beautifully grilled steak that was intended for someone else. No one wants to fail at something. However, the truth of the matter is that you never really fail until you stop trying. If that doesn't ring true to you, then always try to "fail forward." This means that you may have to take imperfect action. This kind of action prevents you from getting stuck at less than 100% perfect action. This sort of growth will help you stretch and become closer to whom you want to be.

As I was walking down that sidewalk, I failed to completely avoid the occasional stumble. But when I did stumble, I didn't fall. Over the years, I've continued to walk and have gotten better about not stumbling. There are still times that make me wonder when a fall will happen. My continuous efforts, for all of these years, deserve to show growth. Wouldn't it be great if we could all look at our lives and see our own growth? Too many times we don't see it because we're caught up the day-in, day-out running from task to task.

If you can summarize what the **D** in D.R.E.A.M. stands for, it would have to be *deserving*, because you are deserving of the right to dream. You already have the ability; you just need to give yourself the time. In order to effectively dream, you may need to take a personal day that's really personal. You will need to spend time working on YOU. Once you have committed to that, it'll be much easier to accomplish the task at hand. And remember, the task is for you to dream.

The second reason that people have a hard time chasing their dreams is that they're afraid of succeeding. That's right, they're afraid that if they chase their dreams, they'll be forced to change who they are. They may be forced to give up certain luxuries, friends, or habits. As Johnny Depp once said, "Success doesn't change you, it reveals you." Think about what you would do if your dreams came true. Now, without getting into the individual steps, think about what needs to happen for you to live your dream.

This recently happened to me, when I dreamed of the day when I could start my own business. At the time, I was in Information Technology sales. My degree was in Industrial Engineering, but I had this huge hole in my heart where I dreamt of helping other people that were struggling with adversity. Helping other people with the gifts that I've been given has always been important to me. Then, one by one, obstacles that were in the path of my dream were removed. My dream suddenly became possible. There are many factors that went into that happening, not the least of which was constant and repetitive prayer.

Now what? There's an awful lot of work to do. It's one thing to change your mind. It's quite another to change your work habits, your income — not to mention your career.

The **R** in D.R.E.A.M. stands for *reinforcements* because of how important they are as we strive for our dreams. There are so many times that we'll need them, whether good or bad, but they are crucial. You need to have reinforcements. People who know your dreams and desires, and who will support you as you pursue those dreams. With them, your chances of achieving your dreams will be much greater.

I'm fortunate to have a huge group of supporters behind me for reinforcement. They know my story and how passionate I am to be successful. They could never have a full appreciation for what all of this means to me, but seeing the impact on others will make it much more apparent.

As you go through this process of learning how to dream, you'll experience different things. It's important to remember as many of those things as possible. You may want to start a journal. It's not so much that you'll want it to refer back to, but writing things down will help them to soak into your memory.

To continue on with the acronym, the **E** stands for *experience*. It doesn't mean that if we've been in sales all of our life, the only experiences that we're going to have are going to be sales-related. That only means the lens we look through, at times, will have a salesperson's perspective. There are so many other times that we come into contact with people whom we can impact and who have an impact on us. It wouldn't be right to just let it go by without committing this to memory by writing it down. These experiences deserve to be remembered.

Looking back, I can remember taking notes during all of my meetings. Many times, I did go back to them for reference. But, even if I didn't, they still served as the foundation for so many relationships that I have to this day. Maybe it's because writing things down helped me to remember more about people's stories. Maybe it's because they saw me writing things down during every meeting and were more committed to the relationship because they could physically see my commitment.

For whatever the reason, documenting your experiences is always a good idea. Time-stamping them also provides a great deal of relevance. This way you can associate different events in your life with other events. For example, I was trying to lose weight to start off 2015, but my dad was seriously ill, and I found it difficult to stay on a regimented diet. As I documented my weight every week, my dad's condition never improved, and he ended up passing in April of that year. Coincidentally or not, I was at my highest weight ever at the same time. Then in October of that same year, my mother-in-law suddenly passed away. During that year, I never really thought about it, but looking back there was a definite correlation between my weight gain and the loss of loved ones.

I needed time for that set of circumstances to end and then become more rooted in my actions to become healthier. You may have heard it said before that a goal without action is just a dream. That may be true, but it's important that you start somewhere. Once you start, it's important that you stay focused, never losing sight of your dream. It's OK if your dream changes, but always revisit your dream to ensure that your actions are matching a path that would allow you to achieve your dream. This is why the **A** in D.R.E.A.M. stands for *action*.

You'll never be able to accomplish anything in life if you don't do something. Start where you are with who you are. This is your baseline for future growth. You'll be able to come back someday and "remember when." It'll be at these times when you'll be able to see a measurable improvement. Then you'll come to the realization that all of those baby steps and bumps along the way really did matter. You'll also have an appreciation for the peaks and valleys. Trust me, there will be plenty of both of them, but the overall trend will be one of improvement. The graph will show your trend to the upper-right quadrant.

Measurement is the **M** in dream because it's important to take measurements to show our growth. With the evidence of growth, we'll be more motivated to keep on the same path, especially during the times when you find yourself in one of the valleys. Those are tough times for all of us, but without a baseline measurement, the road can seem endless.

As I sit here thinking about the person reading these words, I think of how much they could achieve. I think about how I could have structured this book differently. I think about all those voices that told me that I couldn't do it. I think of all of those people who said, "What do you have to say?" Or "Who do you think would want to read that?" With my baseline and measurements, I can confidently show them my improvement. Not to say, "I told you so," but to show them that with the will of the human spirit, it can be done. And, yes, I did it.

The only problem with this is that you have to suck first. You're not going to come out of the gate and achieve your dreams in the first month. If you do, your dreams aren't big enough. This is a difficult aspect of self-im-provement. You have to be understanding when someone tells you that you've got a long way to go. You have got to be understanding when someone tells you, "let me know when you get good." You have got to be understanding when you show someone the progress that you've made in achieving your goal and they say, "that's a good start."

When you assign actions and dates to your dreams, they will become goals.

CHAPTER 11

CHART YOUR COURSE — ENVISION YOUR PLAN[2]

Once I had set my course to go down that sidewalk in downtown Columbus, I knew that I had the tools to get me to my destination. These are the tools that I have with me every day. There are many tools to be used and ways that you can allow yourself or your organization to carry on with the same attitude, work ethic, and belief system. Here are some examples of these tools.

Be an Encourager

You should always be a source of encouragement. That doesn't mean beating people into submission, it means leading them when they are weak and vulnerable. It also

---

[2] Much of this chapter is drawn from the teaching in Kary Oberbrunner's book *The Deeper Path*. Some of the text and most of the concepts in this chapter are his, used with permission.

means leading them when they are strong and confident. There are always teaching moments in each aspect. A true encourager never speaks a negative word about his team in a public setting. Your approach in private always has a positive slant. It allows the receiver of the positive criticism to understand where they are possibly in the wrong.

Be a Truth Teller

Surrounding yourself with people that always encourage and tell you that you're doing a good job isn't helpful either. It's important to have someone feeding you with information about things that may be lurking in your blind spot. These truth tellers can also be an encourager, but their pragmatic approach convinces you that they're not always there to lift you up, but they're sometimes there to light you up. Being lit up, in a good way, is something that we all need from time to time. It shows how others are affected by our thoughts, words, and actions.

Keep in mind that you may have to pay someone to be effective in this role, because many leaders are uncomfortable doing this. Yet many times an organization or person needs the truth in order to move forward.

Keep Them Hungry

It's important to give people a taste of what success is like. They need to understand what the fruits of efforts look like. It's critical that they also see how you handle success. At the same time, you want to make sure that they understand that the rewards of your hard work are *your* rewards. That doesn't mean that they can't share in it, but they need to come to the realization that they need to have their own success. Then they'll be able to experience their own rewards. The good news is that this will show them that a process is in place to have their own moment. Now, the brass ring is theirs to grab.

Keep Them Engaged

You won't need to work that hard to keep true leaders engaged. However, you need to continue to reinforce that they are leaders of today and tomorrow. Without that, they'll be inclined to take their skills elsewhere. You need to continue to invest in them, so they continue to invest in you. Without a reciprocal business relationship, your leaders will be leaners. You'll find them leaning on their shovels, leaning on their desks, and leaning on their laurels.

Keeping leaders engaged will vary from person to person. There is no one cure-all to maintain leadership engagement.

Develop Everyone's Leadership Skills

This seems to be the intangible result that everyone is looking for. There's no mistaking why that is. It's because these people will determine the future. In essence, they will be running the planet after our time has passed. In our last remaining years and after we're gone, we'll want them to have the skills to lead forward. There are so many leadership programs out there. You may be wondering which one to choose. This is a valid concern, but not one that should stop you. After you've done some research, pick a program and USE IT! If, in the future, you determine that there is a better program, then you can always switch programs. You will have nothing to regret in acting now.

Stretch Them — Make Them Uncomfortable

A friend of mine once told me how he had been with his banking company for some time and had gone through an MBA program to help him get to the next level. He was anxious for the move, because he knew that it meant a reward for all of his hard work over the recent years. Oddly enough, he was given a different position. He became a bank teller on the front line. You see, management saw his leadership skills, but also understood that he needed to be stretched. He needed to understand the concerns of the customer on the front lines. He had to have an appreciation for what bank tellers go through on a daily basis. Once he DID get the promotion to the higher position, he had a much better idea of how his decisions would have a lasting impact on his coworkers and customers company-wide.

Be Self-Aware

It all starts here. Clear your mind of preconceived notions. Clear your mind of outside voices. Clear your mind of third-party thoughts. Clear your mind of your next question. How do you do that? In times of conflict it's difficult, but it will be easier if you make time to prepare. The more time that you prepare for a conversation, the greater the chances are that you'll be in a position to listen effectively. It's called active listening. It comes with thought and preparation.

Here's a tip: when you know that you have a meeting coming up, write that person's name on a piece of paper. Below their name, whenever a topic comes to mind that you want to be sure to cover, write it down under that person's name. This will allow you to formulate questions and an agenda for your meeting. I recall doing this at IBM and remember how much in control it made me feel. And you know, if I was feeling it, I'm sure that the other person was feeling it. They felt my confidence and thoughtfulness. They probably even thought that I was smarter than I am.

There is no Hansel and Gretel "breadcrumb" path to get to your vision. It's not going to be that easy. However, if you go back to the previous chapter and reflect on your dream, you will see results if you remain intentional in your efforts to accomplish it. Like anything in life, the greater your focus and unending attention, the greater your chances will be of successful achieving your dream. If you take detours and go down rabbit holes, results are not as sure. There are many times that we get distracted and lose sight. This is where we need to go back to building our core to regain our vision.

> There is no Hansel and Gretel "breadcrumb" path to get to your vision.

Writing this book required me to focus and build my core. It's part of my O.P.U.S., which is essentially the masterpiece of one's life. It's part of my dream. It's part of me.

Most big dreams include three main ingredients. Not identifying them would be regrettable, since you'll need to have this knowledge for the next time that you dream.

- Some<u>one</u> (Tribe) — Who is needed to make your dream a reality?

- Some<u>thing</u> (Cause) — What is the cause that you're working toward?
- Some<u>where</u> (Space) — Where do you plan to live out this dream?

When you think about writing your own O.P.U.S., it's easiest to put it in these terms. Keep your dream in mind as you write. The time that you spend writing is where you'll determine much more about yourself than you ever could have thought. Not only does writing help you to understand your own thoughts, but it also helps to cement those thoughts. The importance of that will become evident when you have conversations with other people. Having that conversation will be much more comfortable.

In the literal sense, *opus* means a song or lyric that represents your life's work. This can be stretched to mean the work that you've done and the melody line that you've been communicating to others as you've gone through life. Understanding your O.P.U.S. is something that is critical once you've established your dream. Your dream will give you the ability to start writing your O.P.U.S..

Before we do that, let's go back to the 20 "I believe" statements that you wrote at the end of Chapter 9. Understanding and revisiting your belief systems, coupled with your dreams will make this process much easier.

All of the steps that I took on the sidewalk in downtown Columbus had meaning. Without them, I wouldn't have been able to get where I was going. Without them, I would have been stuck. Without them, I'm not sure where I'd be. When I was able to determine my location and preferred destination, I was able to piece together what it would take me to get there. For all intents and purposes, my O.P.U.S. was written that day.

It can best be remembered as follows:

Overarching Vision. This is your big chance to tell it like you dream it would be. Remember Martin Luther King's "I have a dream" speech? Notice, that he didn't say "I have a plan" or "I have a thought." Plans and thoughts don't inspire people, but dreams do.

For example, my overarching vision is for people to embrace their own personal blindness to achieve vision.

> Plans and thoughts don't inspire people, but dreams do.

When you write yours, after you read this, don't worry about other people's opinion. Be as open as you possibly can. Don't think about the reasons why it may or may not be possible. Just let it go. This will allow you to declutter your mind and help you to get your dream on paper.

Purpose. This is the defining statement for your work. This is generally one sentence that sums up your work. What is that you feel God has put you on earth to do? Great artists have the ability to create new work that is instantly recognizable as theirs, without them even signing it. Critics and admirers know that it's their work because of how it was constructed. Can you say that about your life? When someone says, "I'm wondering who can help me or offer me advice" in a certain area, are people apt to think of you? If they don't think of you, when your name is mentioned is there an obvious, "Oh, yeah" moment?

Unifying Strategies. What does that mean? Different actions or directions that are brought together for one purpose. These are necessary for you to achieve your Overarching Vision. It's important that you understand that you don't want too many strategies to begin with, so that's why you are going to condense it down to a handful. This will simplify your life greatly and allow you to stay focused.

Having that focus is one of the main reasons for writing your own O.P.U.S., because once you do that you'll be able to knock out the clutter in your life. Having done this, you know when you have permission from yourself to cut things out or drop them off your calendar.

Scorecard for Success. So, how are you doing? Let's let you be the judge as you begin to assimilate all of this information and take small steps to achieve your dream. This scorecard will essentially correlate with the Unifying Strategies as they are categories for where you will be spending your efforts. This Scorecard will lend itself to the content for each of those strategies.

You can set it up in whatever way is most effective for you. For the sake of simplicity, I keep a calendar that shows what I have scheduled. I can then take that and compare it to what has been accomplished. It's important that you keep it simple. This has to be something that you can do at a glance.

This will be representative of the different milestones that you reach along the way. If you have a handful of Unifying Strategies, your Scorecard for Success should mirror those. When it comes time to begin to track this information, you'll be able to align them for future reference.

As we've talked about in earlier chapters, it's important to build your core. For that reason, our O.P.U.S. can't take us far without our Core Six-Pack. This, much like the O.P.U.S., comes from the *Deeper Path Book* by Kary Oberbrunner.

1. Worldview — What I Believe
2. Identity — Who I Am
3. Principles — What I Value
4. Passion — What I Love
5. Purpose — Why I Live and Work
6. Process — How Will I Do It

You'll first need to write out your "Worldview," or put another way, "how do you view the world." Start each sentence with "I believe...."

The next step is to process your Identity. Start each sentence with "I am..."

Principles are what makes your life have true worth. Start each sentence with "I value..."

"Passion" or what you love is the next thing that you'll need to put down. Start each statement with "I love..."

The next step is one that people can get caught on. If you need help, please send me a note. Think of this as your "why" statement. Start each Purpose sentence with "I live to" or "I help."

You won't be able to do this effectively without a "Process" or "How will you do it?" This is called our Playbook of Productive Action (or POP). Beginning with today, look at your month, and organize the next four weeks based on your Unifying Strategies.

As an example, here is my O.P.U.S. Use this as an example of what to include in yours.

My Purpose

Offer hope for people who may have sight, but not vision, to embrace blindness.

My Tribe

Imagine a tribe of people that are in need of vision and those that are able to help to people along the way.

My Cause

Imagine a world where people embrace what having blindness can mean to achieve vision.

My Space

Imagine a place where the distractions and chaos of the world are quieted, which allows you to focus on what is truly important.

Unifying Strategies

Personal Growth — By investing in myself, I will be able to invest in others. With anything in life, you can't expect to get out more than what you put in.

What I will use:

* Words (content) — Investing time in consuming and digesting content that challenges my paradigms
* Thoughts (relationships) — Learning from teachers, mentors, and coaches who stretch my thinking because of their own commitment to personal growth
* Deeds (Experiences) — Engaging in experiences even though they might be uncomfortable, unfamiliar, or unchartered

Mutually Beneficial Relationships — By connecting and collaborating with mentors and mentees, I'll be able to live out my story of going from Blindness to Sight to Vision.

* Tribe — I will build a tribe committed to building themselves and finding hope
* Cause — I will identify entry points for people to consider and commit to the cause
* Space — I will design locations (virtual and physical) that enable transformation to take place

Platform — By sharing my story via books, editorials, and speaking engagements, I will have an opportunity to share my story of hope and give it to others.

* Writing blog stories and books that will enable workshop conversations
* Speaking with, or to, anyone who will listen
* Confidence in my words will allow me to answer their questions appropriately

Group Development — By fostering relationships and the formation of "Like Minds," these groups will form their own identities based on needs.

* Personal Advisory Committee that is formed to encourage and guide me for the purpose of inspiring hope

Transformation Experiences — By becoming more believable and by believing in others, I'm qualified to create spaces that invite and challenge others to get and give hope.

* Teaching in sharing information
* Mentoring in sharing experience
* Consulting in sharing advice
* Training in sharing skills
* Coaching in sharing transformation
* Counseling in sharing therapy
* Author in sharing inspiration

My Core Six-Pack

This consists of:

1. Worldview — What I Believe

I believe that the glory of God is right in front of us.

I believe that my father is in heaven with my Heavenly Father watching over us.

I believe Jesus lived and then died on the cross, so that he could be an example for us, so that we might live.

I believe that love really does conquer all.

I believe that God answers prayers when the time is right.

I believe that God has a divine plan for me and for my wife and children.

I believe that God is bigger than we could ever imagine and will reveal Himself to many people through me and my family.

I believe that God will be revealed to millions of people who never would have heard of Him.

I believe that most people will go through life never understanding or wanting to understand something that I'm so fortunate to understand.

I believe that everyone has to go blind, at least figuratively, before they can have vision.

I believe that everyone believes in something — they may as well believe in the truth.

I believe that God has called me to tell my story to people that are hurting and struggling to overcome obstacles in life.

I believe that my hardship and struggles are part of the plan for me to bring more people closer to Christ.

I believe that implementing the Truth in my teachings doesn't have to mean quoting scripture and verse.

I believe that I need to be grounded in the Word.

I believe that I need to spend more time in prayer and devotions.

I believe that I have much to learn about scripture and the presence of God's love.

I believe that I am blessed with the outward appearance that makes my purpose, here on earth, easy to understand.

I believe that the hardest thing in life is understanding that life is the hardest thing.

I believe that I'm an arrow in God's quiver that is ready for the enemy.

I believe I'm broken and at times unworthy of God's love, because I am a sinner.

I believe that God's plan for me is bigger than I can fathom.

2. Identity — Who I Am

* I am a Christian who loves God.
* I am a husband and father.
* I am chosen to live out my O.P.U.S. (purpose).
* I am an inspiration to others because of how I live my life.
* I am broken but not broke.
* I am a giver of hope through my life.
* I am a servant leader working for the good of others.
* I am a student of life and eternity.
* I am a boy in a man's body.

3. Principles — What I Value

* I value people that only have one face.
* I value recreation in all everything that I do.
* I value quiet time.
* I value the smell of a baby.

* I value children.
* I value my eyesight.
* I value my life.

4. Passion — What I Love
* I love my wife because we were made for each other.
* I love my kids because they are part of me, and I'm part of them.
* I love my God every day of the week.
* I love being in control at times where I know the lay of the land.
* I love being led at times of unfamiliarity.
* I love asking questions because it's impossible to learn when I'm talking.
* I love listening to other people's stories and answers to my questions.
* I love to laugh...loud.

5. Purpose — Why I Live and Work
* I live to serve others.
* I work to support my family.
* I live so that others can be inspired to do great things.
* I live to make others laugh.
* I live to love and be loved by my family and friends.
* I live to impact those that will hear my story.

6. Process — How Will I Do It
* I will do this with the daily discipline of taking action
* I will consult with people I trust
* I will reach out to people in need
* I will invest in other people
* I will give my time where needed

CHAPTER 12

CHART YOUR JOURNEY —
ENVISION YOUR SIDEWALK

I t takes a village. No one expects you to do this alone. Building your dream, like building your core, is tough work. This is where you'll need to step out of your bubble and, quite possibly, become uncomfortable. Experience what others have done before you. It's not that they've done it perfectly. It's not that their situation is identical. What it is, is another set of eyes — or one eye in my case :-) — to look at your work. Another set of ears to hear your ideas. Another brain to interpret thoughts.

This book started with my story, and it ends with my story. Now that it's about to end, hopefully you've been able to see yourself in these pages.

Being in a leadership position reminds me of when I was on church council. Without question, that's where my faith was firmly rooted in the teachings directly from the Bible. One of the first verses that I recall from those long council meetings is Proverbs 27:17: "As iron sharpens iron, so one man sharpens another." That verse made me think of all of the people that have had such a great influence in my faith journey.

I've had a chance to share with those people what they've meant to me. That's probably been the most interesting part of all of this. I've been able to meet with CEOs and presidents of organizations and tell them of the impact that they've had on my life. It didn't matter what my level was in the organization or where I came from. They were all accepting of me and willing to share their faith journey.

Leaders are believers.

In addition, I've gotten to know many people who are in different stages of life. Some of the most poignant conversations have been with people who have cancer. They know their own circumstances and they're not always mad about it. I'm not sure what to say about all of these people other than they have had an impact on my life, and I would encourage you to let them have an impact on your life as well.

In the end, that's what it's really all about. It's about building healthy relationships and allowing others to have an impact on you. Positive impact is good impact. How do you know what positive impact looks like? That's dependent on your own situation, but it doesn't come from any electronic device, bottle, or magazine. You can control your thoughts by controlling what goes into your mind. It's up to you and the outside forces that you allow into your life.

No one said that this was easy. If it were easy, it wouldn't seem worth it, and you'd be less apt to do it. If it were easy, the pains that you go through wouldn't last as long and wouldn't stay in your memory as long. If they don't stay in your memory, you're less likely to carry them with you. Carrying them with you day after day is a constant reminder of where you came from. It's a constant reminder of the success that you've already achieved and will be an incentive for how you can achieve more.

When you get to the end of your sidewalk, what would you like to have happen? Would you want to just continue walking? It's not going to hurt anything.

> When you get to the end of your sidewalk, what would you like to have happen?

There's only a risk that you may miss out on something. There's always going to be a chance that you could've done more. When you get to the end of the sidewalk, you don't want to be filled with regret. You'll want to know that you've lived a full life. You'll want to know that you've made a difference.

When you get to the end of the sidewalk, who do you think will be standing next to you? Every time that I looked up, when I was on my journey, I could see Connie. She worries about me constantly and I give her good reason to. I can't sit still and work a 8-to-5 job, come home at the end of the day and relax. She's even worse about that than I am, but that doesn't keep her from worrying. It doesn't matter what your situation is. Who's worried about you?

Will there be another piece of sidewalk for you at the end of this one? Where do you think it will lead? How long do you think that you'll have to get there? Will you have companionship? Do you need directions?

These are some deep questions. How can you answer them all? How can you understand them all? When do you get to experience the joy of completing your walk? These are questions that we all have to answer ourselves.

We love to help people embrace their own blindness to achieve a greater vision for their lives. We'd love for you to connect with us, explore our resources, and find out how we can help you, your business, or your group.

Visit our website at ARadicalVision.com

If you'd like to go deeper, I'd love to hear from you. Please reach out to me in one of the following ways.

email: brian@ARadicalVision.com
phone: (614) 946-1635
Twitter: @aradicalvision
Facebook: A Radical Vision
LinkedIn: A Radical Vision

Sometimes it *DOES* take a brain surgeon, but my hope is that you don't need one.

ACKNOWLEDGEMENTS

My mom and dad are responsible for me making it into this world and then shaping me. Even though dad is in heaven, I still love you both.

This book took a year to write. It took 50 years of experience. More than all of that, it took a marriage of 26 years. That's a long time to put up with me and my crazy ideas. As I write these words, my wife still hasn't read the first word of the book. She doesn't have to, because she has lived it. This book has more to do with her than it does me. She's the real story here. I love you, Connie.

When I told my kids four years ago at Cracker Barrel in Hilliard, Ohio that I was going to write a book, they said "that's awesome!" I'm sure that they don't remember that occasion, but I do. Grant, Jess, and Colin, I love you all more than you can imagine. You're the most amazing people that I know.

Pastor Warren Reichert, who started me on this journey is the late 1990s.

My professional editor, Andrea Clute. This book is so much better since it's been touched by you.

Thank you to my friends Bill Brown and Kevin Rall for encouraging me to write this book 6 years ago.

My "friend" editors enabled me to pick this book back up when I wanted to quit. It's a good thing that they didn't know that. :-) Bill Brown, Bill Ehrman, Mark Tremayne,

Ken Neff, and JD Biros. Ken and JD, you've endured more than your share of me banging my head on the table. It's interesting that only Bill Brown knew me when I had two good eyes. You're all awesome.

I'm thankful for Earl Osborne, Pete Miller, Jeff Sopp, Rye D'Orazio, and Bill Brown. These are people that God put into my life in the late '90s.

Thank you to my coach and mentor Kary Oberbrunner who is truly a gift sent from God. The people who are blessed to know you understand the value you bring and the blessing you are. Thanks for believing in me.

Thank you to Mark Henson, owner of sparkspace and author of *Ordinary Superpowers*. Your friendship has been incredible. I appreciate you making me feel worthy.

Thank you to all of the people who have encouraged me along the way to write this book.

Many times people say that there are too many people to mention who have helped them, and that is true. However, they can usually list their closest family members that have helped. Fortunately, I am blessed with too many brothers, sisters, in-laws, nieces, nephews, etc., to mention, but they've all played a part.

This book was written in coffee shops all across Hilliard, Ohio. Not to mention my basement office and locations where my mind wandered without a pen & paper, laptop, or smartphone. The thoughts became glued to my brain until the time was right. Hilliard has been a beautiful place to raise our family over the last 22 years. Thank you.

Thanks for being my best friend Eric and John.

Thanks for being my prayer warrior Norm.